not a guide to
Plymouth

E. Locke & M. Richards

The History Press

First published 2012

The History Press
The Mill, Brimscombe Port
Stroud, Gloucestershire, GL5 2QG
www.thehistorypress.co.uk

British Library Cataloguing in Publication Data.
A catalogue record for this book is available from the British Library.

ISBN 978 0 7524 7777 0

Typesetting and origination by The History Press
Printed in Great Britain

TURRIS FORTISSIMA EST NOMEN JEHOVA

We would like to thank our mum, Marilyn, for her help with some of the more obscure information on Plymouth in this book. She is a true Plymothian through and through.

Contents

4

Plymouth

Pronounced /**plɪməθ**/

Built between the mouths of the rivers Plym to the east and Tamar to the west, where they join Plymouth Sound, since 1967 the city has included the suburbs of Plympton and Plymstock, which are on the east side of the River Plym.

Plymouth's history goes back to the Bronze Age, when its first settlement grew at Mount Batten. This settlement continued to grow as a trading post for the Roman Empire, until the more prosperous village of Sutton, the current Plymouth, surpassed it.

Grid Reference

8

Ordnance Survey grid reference: SX 48150 55062

Street Names

Here's a selection of quirky street names from around the city . . .

Blue Haze Close

Dark Street Lane

Dark Lake View

Diamond Avenue

Drunken Bridge Hill

Eastern Kings

Firestone Close

Gun Lane

Jump Close

Linketty Lane

Little Fancy Close

Lizard Walk

Long Ley

Marrowbone Slip

Memory Lane

Moon Cove

Old Laundry

Paradise Place

Paton Watson Quadrate

Pepper Lane

Periwinkle Drive

Pin Lane

Pleasure Hill

Rifleman Walk

Six O'Clock Lane

Terra Nova Green

Unicorn Close

Yonder Street

. . . and some quirky area names:

Camel's Head

Eggbuckland

Ham

Mutley

Pennycomequick

Pennycross

Plymouth Ward Snapshots

Budshead – acquired its name from the Breton St Budoc, who is said to have come to the area in AD 480 to form a small religious community. Budshead Wood Local Nature Reserve is located here.

Compton – once a small village, Compton was developed in the 1930s and now lies between the suburbs of Mannamead and Efford. There are two parts, Higher and Lower Compton, named after two farms and now distinguished by their respective public houses, the Rising Sun at Higher Compton, and the Compton Inn at Lower Compton. As their names imply, Higher Compton is geographically higher than Lower Compton. Lower Compton was home to the late painter Robert Lenkiewicz.

Devonport – formerly Plymouth Dock or just Dock, originally one of the Three Towns (along with Plymouth and East Stonehouse) which merged in 1914 to form what would become in 1928 the city of Plymouth. Home to Plymouth's naval base.

Drake – contains the University of Plymouth campus, Drake's Leat, railway station, Museum & Art Gallery, Central Library, Drake Circus shopping centre. Suffered a fatal bomb explosion during the Plymouth Blitz.

Efford and Lipson – a large and mostly post-war suburb, on high ground above the Laira estuary. Contains Efford Fort, Freedom Fields Park, Civil War battlesite, the site of Plymouth's former hospital (Freedom Fields Hospital, now demolished), fire and ambulance stations, Lipson Community College, Efford Marsh Nature Reserve.

Eggbuckland – mentioned in the Domesday Book as being granted to the Saxon Heche or Ecca, thus the land was known as Ecca's Bocheland. Held by royalist cavaliers during the Civil War. Residential area. Eggbuckland Community College is located here.

Ham – post-war suburb named after the seventeenth-century Ham House, home of the Trelawney family. Close to the dockyard and naval base as well as the A38 Devon Expessway. Ham Woods are in this ward.

Honicknowle – residential area, previously part of Knackersnowle. Borders with West Park, Crownhill, Ham, Whitleigh and Pennycross.

Moor View – this seat is largely the successor to the former Devonport constituency.

Peverell – named in the Domesday Book, this ward contains Edwardian terraced houses, Central Park, Plymouth Argyle Football Club.

Plympton Chaddlewood / Plympton Erle / Plympton St Mary – mentioned in the Domesday Book and site of a priory founded in the twelfth century. The ancient stannary town remains dominated by the now ruined Norman motte-and-bailey castle. Birthplace and residence of painter Joshua Reynolds, who was Mayor of Plympton as well as first president of the Royal Academy of Art. Home to the Plym Valley Railway – a preserved railway based at the reconstructed Marsh Mills station on Coypool Road. Today it is a populous, north-eastern suburb of the city of Plymouth, of which it officially became part, along with Plymstock, in 1967, although it still has its own town centre (called the Ridgeway).

15

Plymstock Dunstone / Plymstock Radford – a rural parish which developed quickly before and after the Second World War. Today a populous and mostly home-owning south-eastern suburb of the city. Coombe Dean School and Plymstock School are located here, as is Plymstock Library.

St Budeaux – named after St Budoc (the French pronunciation of St Budoc is St Budeaux), documented in the Domesday Book, bombed during the Second World War – subsequent rebuilding resulted in a housing explosion. Home to a Catholic church, a Methodist church, a Baptist church, two Church of England churches, a public library, three pubs, four primary schools and two railway stations.

St Peter and the Waterfront – home to Plymouth Hoe, Smeaton's Tower, Tinside Pool, the Wheel of Plymouth, elegant period terraces of Victorian and Edwardian houses and hotels.

Southway – a large suburban housing estate in north-west Plymouth. The name is believed to have derived from the route into Plymouth used by Buckland Abbey monks, which was known as the 'South Way'. Southway Community College and Southway Valley Nature Reserve are located here.

Stoke – formerly Stoke Damerel, inner suburb. Stoke Damerel Community College is in this ward.

Sutton and Mount Gould – in a by-election in 1919, Sutton became the first constituency in Great Britain to elect a female MP: Nancy Astor became the first woman to take a seat in the House of Commons. Home to Mount Gould Hospital.

Distance from . . .

Place	Miles	Km
Ayers Rock, Australia	9,518	15,318
Brussels, Belgium	374	602
Centre of the Earth	3,975	6,397
Death Valley, USA	5,198	8,366
Eiffel Tower, Paris	306	494
Frankfurt, Germany	567	912
Glasgow, Scotland	380	612
Hong Kong, China	6,169	9,927
Istanbul, Turkey	1,709	2,750
Jerusalem, Israel	2,380	3,831
The Kremlin, Russia	1,747	2,812
Lima, Peru	6,135	9,873
The Moon (average distance)	384,403	238,857
Niagara Falls, North America	3,436	5,530
Osaka, Japan	6,072	9,772
Panama Canal, Republic of Panama	5,106	8,217
Queenstown, New Zealand	11,953	19,236
Reykjavik, Iceland	1,152	1,854
Syracuse, Sicily	1,330	2,141
The Taj Mahal, India	4,469	7,192
Ural Mountains, Russia	2,510	4,039
Vatican City	984	1,584
Washington DC, USA	3,526	5,675
Xanthi, Greece	1,527	2,457
Yellowstone National Park, USA	4,550	7,323
Zurich, Switzerland	613	986

Twinnings

Brest, France, since 1963
Like Plymouth, Brest is a large university city with a long maritime history. It is an important harbour; a military port; home to the *Académie de Marine* (Naval Academy), which was founded in 1752; and every four years hosts the International Festival of the Sea. Situated on the north-western coast of Brittany, Brest is only 136 miles from Plymouth. Several ferries cross from Plymouth each day and take about 6 hours to reach France. The nearest ferry port to Brest is at Roscoff, 40 miles away.

Gdynia, Poland, since 1976
The city of Gdynia is located on the Polish Baltic Coast. Unlike Plymouth, Gdynia is a relatively modern city, having only been established in 1926. Associations between the two cities, however, date back to the Second World War, with close naval ties and a large expatriate community in Plymouth.

Novorossiysk, Russia, since 1990
The city of Novorossiysk is Russia's most significant Black Sea Port, handling 50 per cent of the country's oil exports, plus timber, coal, grain and cement.The city is recalled in Plymouth by Novorossiysk Road.

San Sebastian, Spain, since 1990
Situated in the Basque region of northern Spain, San Sebastian, like Plymouth, has a rich maritime history and is also a popular centre for sailing.

Plymouth, Massachusetts, USA, since 2001
In June 2001, Plymouth formally cemented one of the oldest municipal links in existence by recognising a connection which began in 1620, when the *Mayflower* set sail from the city carrying the Pilgrim Fathers to the New World.

Welcome
to Plymouth
Twinned with Tonic

HANDS ACROSS THE SEA

COMMEMORATING THE VISIT OF THE PLYMOUTH
MICHIGAN DELEGATION TO ARIZTOWER TO
LET THIS TREE FOREVER BEA SYMBOL OF THE
FRIENDSHIP BETWEEN THE TWO CITIES

JULY 17, 1976

Plymouth International

Plymouth, England, is not alone. The following corners of the world also have Plymouths:

The British Windward Islands has Plymouths in Tobago and Monserrat Island.

Africa has Plymouth Rock.

New Zealand has New Plymouth.

Antarctica has Plymouth Mount.

Considering the Founding Fathers of the United States set sail from Plymouth, the USA naturally has Plymouths all over the place, including: Massachusetts, Worcester County; Pennsylvania, Luzerne County; Michigan, Wayne County; Wisconsin, Sheboygan County; North Carolina, Washington County; New Hampshire, Grafton County; Ohio, Ashtabula County; Florida, Orange County; Washington State, Benton County; Delaware County; Richland County; West Illinois, Hancock County; Southern Maine, Penobscot County; Northern Iowa, Cerro Gordo County; California, Amador County; Nebraska, Jefferson County; Vermont, Windsor County; Northern Utah, Box Edler County; Kansas, Russell County; Texas; West Virginia; Missouri; Minnesota; New York State; North Carolina; New Brunswick; Mississippi, Pontotoc County; Nova Scotia, Yarmouth County; Nova Scotia, Picton County; North Indiana, Marshall County, Connecticut.

Historical Timeline

Plymouth is
given a Charter

Civil War begins and
Plymouth supports
the Parliamentarians

The Plymouth Eye
Dispensary (later
the Royal Eye
Infirmary) opens

The Royal Albert
Bridge is officially
opened by HRH
Prince Albert

English fleet
sails to fight
the Spanish
Armada

Work starts on
the new Naval
Dockyard

Four of the
Tolpuddle
Martyrs sail
into Plymouth
after being
pardoned

Devonport
Prison opens at
Pennycomequick

Hoe Park
opens

1254	1588	1642	1690	1821	1838	1859	1878	1888

1577	1626	1677	1812	1833	1845	1860 –70	1884

Work starts
on Plymouth
Breakwater

Plymouth
Dockyard
becomes
Devonport
Dockyard

The Promenade
Pier is officially
opened by the
Mayor, John
Greenway

Plymouth is
struck by the
plague, with
some 2,000
victims

King Charles
II and Samuel
Pepys visit
Plymouth

Princess Victoria
visits the dockyard,
four years before she
becomes Queen

A line of forts are built
around Plymouth

Drake sets sail on
his circumnavigation
of the world

24

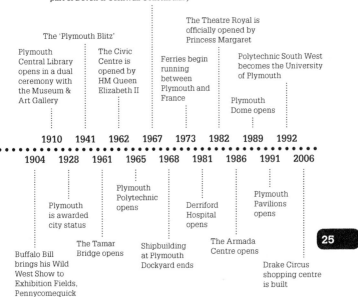

Plymouth City Police are amalgamated with
the neighbouring county forces to become
part of Devon & Cornwall Constabulary

The Theatre Royal is
officially opened by
Princess Margaret

The 'Plymouth Blitz'

Plymouth
Central Library
opens in a dual
ceremony with
the Museum &
Art Gallery

The Civic
Centre is
opened by
HM Queen
Elizabeth II

Ferries begin
running
between
Plymouth and
France

Polytechnic South West
becomes the University
of Plymouth

Plymouth
Dome opens

1910   1941   1962   1967   1973   1982   1989   1992

1904   1928   1961   1965   1968   1981   1986   1991   2006

Plymouth
Polytechnic
opens

Plymouth
is awarded
city status

Derriford
Hospital
opens

Plymouth
Pavilions
opens

The Tamar
Bridge opens

Shipbuilding
at Plymouth
Dockyard ends

The Armada
Centre opens

Buffalo Bill
brings his Wild
West Show to
Exhibition Fields,
Pennycomequick

Drake Circus
shopping centre
is built

Iconic View: Plymouth Seafront

A Day in the Life of the City

0500 – Fish landed at Sutton Harbour, ready for sale and delivery throughout the city

0800 – The first Plymouth to Roscoff ferry leaves Millbay

1000 – Tinside Lido opens for those brave enough to take a dip in the open-air seawater (opens at 12 noon out of season)

1030 – Lectures in full swing at the University of Plymouth

1100 – Feed the sharks at the National Marine Aquarium (Mondays, Wednesdays and Fridays)

1300 – Midday prayer at St Mathias on North Hill

1400 – Hop on the Discovery Tour Bus from the Mayflower Steps to explore the city's heritage

1500 – Plymouth Argyle kick-off at Home Park (Saturdays)

1700 – The last flight of the day leaves Plymouth City Airport for Dublin

1730 – The shopkeepers of Plymouth close up after another busy day

2000 – Curtain goes up on a performance at the Theatre Royal, Plymouth

2030 – Comedians, poets or cabaret performers on stage at the B-Bar on Castle Street

Plymouth in Numbers – Then

43,956 – record attendance at Home Park (Plymouth Argyle *v.* Aston Villa, 10 October 1936)

264,000 – number of visitors to the National Marine Aquarium in 2010

£81,000 – average property price for a terraced house in Plymouth in 2002

£200m – cost of the redevelopment of Drake Circus in 2004

£1.1m – cost to build Plymouth Civic Centre, which was opened by the Queen in 1962

420ft – length of the Promenade Pier on Plymouth Hoe

2 p.m. – the time that the *Western Evening Herald* was launched as Plymouth's first evening newspaper on 22 April 1895

88 – the number of the first bus to leave Bretonside bus station when it opened on 30 March 1958

1849 – the first railway station in Plymouth opened at Millbay

£300,000 – cost to build Plymouth Zoo in 1962

11.13 a.m. – the time of the solar eclipse on 11 August 1999. Sightseers flocked to the Hoe to watch the spectacle

2*s* 6*d* – the price of a seat in the stalls when the New Palace Theatre of Varieties in Union Street opened in 1898

1945 – Plymouth's last tram left Old Town Street for Peverell Corner on 29 September

1910 – the City Museum & Art Gallery and the Central Library were both officially opened in a joint ceremony on 25 October

£391 16*s* – the amount raised by subscription to build the organ for St Andrew's Church

201,775 – population of the Three Towns (Plymouth, Stonehouse and Devonport) in 1901

Plymouth in Numbers – Now

01752 – Plymouth area code

97 – number of schools in Plymouth

1,100 – number of beds at Derriford Hospital

1,281 – number of allotments in Plymouth

1,315 – number of people the Theatre Royal can seat

2,500 – number of civilian and service personnel employed at the city's largest employer, HMNB Devonport

21,000 tons – largest Royal Navy ship based at Devonport Dockyard (HMS *Ocean*)

30,000 – University of Plymouth's student population

256,700 – population of Plymouth

750 – number of listed buildings in Plymouth

37 – number of Scheduled Ancient Monuments in Plymouth, the majority of which are connected with the defence of the city

60,800 m² (654,000 ft²) – the floor space at Drake Circus shopping centre

1,270 – number of parking spaces at Drake Circus shopping centre

31,803 – the circulation of the *Plymouth Evening Herald*

14 – number of storeys at the Civic Centre

506 – number of households listed in the telephone directory with the surname Smith

50,000 – number of books available to borrow at Plymouth Central Library

40,000 – number of vehicles which cross the Tamar Bridge each day

1540 – the date the Minerva Inn was built in Looe Street, making it Plymouth's oldest pub

THEATRE.ROYAL

Minerva Inn

Oldest pub in Plymouth Circa 1540

Demographics

How big?
79.29 sq. km (30.6 sq. miles)

How many people?
240,720

Male – **117,571**

Female – **123,149**

aged 0–24 = **77,825**

aged 25–59 = **112,799**

aged 60–74 = **31,533**

aged 75+ = **18,563**

Mirroring national statistics, 51 per cent of the Plymouth population are female, 49 per cent male.

Single people who have never married – **58,477**

Married or remarried – **93,726**

Separated or divorced – **24,774**

Widowed – **16,720**

Ethnicity
White – **27,667**

Largest minority ethnic group: Chinese – **685**

Religion
Christian – **177,068**

No religion – **43,976**

Muslim – **883**

Buddhist – **470**

Hindu – **215**

Jewish – **182**

Sikh – **58**

Other – **701**

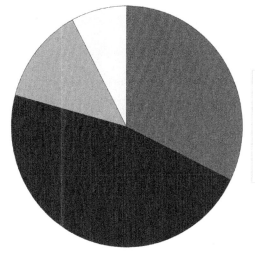

aged 0-24
aged 25-59
aged 60-74
aged 75+

35

Making Headlines

'Disposal experts detonate Plymouth WWII bomb at sea', November 2010

An unexploded Second World War bomb was unearthed by a workman on a site in Notte Street, near Plymouth Hoe. Neighbouring buildings were evacuated, including the Holiday Inn and the Duke of Cornwall Hotel, and a 300m exclusion zone put in place. An estimated 190 people were taken to Plymouth Pavilions sports centre.

The 70kg German wartime bomb, which was 18in long, was stabilised by the MoD Explosive Ordnance Disposal team before being moved to Millbay and taken offshore.

'Second city evacuation as WWII bomb found on demolition site', February 2011

A second Second World War bomb was discovered by a demolition contractor on the same building site in Notte Street where another explosive device was discovered in November 2010. A 100m cordon was set up and properties in Notte Street, Hoe Street and Zion Street were evacuated by police, plus the city's Holiday Inn, which had around 235 guests at the time. As before, Royal Navy bomb disposal experts worked on making the device safe before it was taken to Millbay Docks to be detonated.

'Spiders attack flats in Plymouth', December 2007

Residents had to be evacuated from a block of flats in Plymouth after it was infested by spiders from the black widow family. Called 'false widows', the creatures were spotted running around stairwells near homes. Pest controllers were called in to get rid of the spiders. Resident Gareth Williams, twenty-five, said, 'It was very disturbing.'

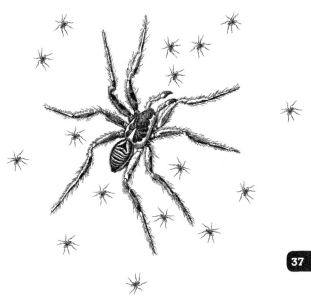

Museums

City Museum & Art Gallery
Built in 1907–10, Plymouth City Museum & Art Gallery in the Drake Circus area, opposite the university, is the city's largest museum and art gallery. The interior of this modern building was restored in 1954 after being gutted in the Blitz and today it houses a diverse collection of exhibits including fine and decorative art, and human and natural history, as well as having space for temporary exhibitions. The museum runs a great regular programme of events, and also has a shop and a café.

Elizabethan House
The Elizabethan House at 32 New Street, the Barbican, was built in 1580 for a sea captain and today still retains many of its historically rare features, including the timber frames, original windows, beams and a spiral staircase winding around an old ship's mast. Inside, this three-storey house is furnished with period furniture, replica soft furnishings and objects related to seafaring including a spice cabinet and old maps.

Merchant's House
Built in 1608 at 33 St Andrew Street, one of Plymouth's oldest roads, this historic four-storey building is the city's finest surviving example of a late sixteenth, early seventeenth-century residence. Privateer and merchant William Parker, a friend of Sir Francis Drake, was the first recorded owner of the house. Mayor of Plymouth from 1601–02, during the seventeenth century it was also home to Plymouth Mayors Justinian Peard and William Symons. Today, the Merchant's House exhibits include a Victorian schoolroom, an Edwardian pharmacy and a room about the Plymouth Blitz and the rebuilding of the city.

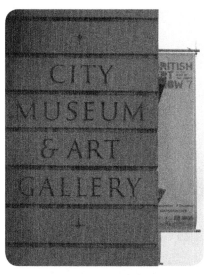

Buildings and Architecture

The Roland Levinsky building, University of Plymouth
Completed in 2007, the building houses the university's Arts and Architecture Faculties. It is named after Professor Roland Levinsky, who was vice chancellor until his tragic death on 1 January 2007.

Dingles
Dingles department store in Armada Way was one of the earliest post-war department stores to open in Britain, and the first in the South West to be fitted with escalators. Opening on 1 September 1951, there were originally three storeys but a fourth was added to the building in 1960.

In December 1988, a serious fire completely destroyed the upper storeys and badly damaged the rest of the store, causing £13.2m worth of damage. A nationwide police hunt was started after extremists targeted five House of Fraser stores as part of an anti-fur campaign, using incendiary bombs. The Plymouth store came off worst, and over 100 firemen were called to tackle the inferno. The store was refurbished and the top two floors rebuilt by 1989.

The Palace Theatre
Originally called the New Palace Theatre of Varieties when it opened as a music hall in Union Street in 1898, it was damaged by fire only eight months later and didn't reopen until May 1899. Artists who appeared on stage here included Harry Houdini in 1909 and Charlie Chaplin in 1931.

The theatre stayed open during the Blitz of 1941 but closed in 1954 due to a lack of touring shows. In 1983 it became the Academy nightclub. Today this Grade II listed building remains closed and its shabby appearance hides its varied history.

The Fresher and Professor
Situated near the university on Gibbon Street, this student pub (its name and the fact that it has a car on the roof gives it away) is a good place to grab a few drinks before heading for Plymouth's nightlife. Try the Terminator – it's pink, yet potent.

Goodbody's, Mutley Plain
Another pub with a car on its roof, this late-night jazz and cabaret bar offers a mellow atmosphere and friendly faces. Beer is served in ice-glazed glasses and a cocktail menu is available. A pub quiz is held every Wednesday night at 9 p.m.

The Duke of Cornwall Hotel
Built in the Victorian Gothic style, the hotel opened on Millbay Road in 1865 to cater for the increasing number of travellers who were coming to the region by rail and sea. The hotel survived the Plymouth Blitz without damage and was the venue for regular functions throughout the Second World War. Today this Grade II listed building is considered to be one of Plymouth's principal landmarks.

Tamar Bridge
This major road bridge linking Devon and Cornwall reached its half century in 2011. Work on the bridge began in 1959 and it was officially opened by Queen Elizabeth the Queen Mother in 1961, at which time it was the longest suspension bridge in the UK. To celebrate the opening, residents were given the chance to walk across the Tamar Bridge before the first car was allowed on it. Located above the Hamoaze, the Tamar Bridge runs parallel to Isambard Kingdom Brunel's Royal Albert Bridge, which opened in 1859.

The Egyptian House, Devonport
The Oddfellows' Hall (better known as the Egyptian House) was designed by John Foulson and built in 1823 at a cost of about £1,500. It still has its original window surrounds and doors complete with Egyptian motifs. In 1867 it was purchased by the Oddfellows but by the 1870s the building was the property of the congregation of Mount Zion. Today the building is a social club.

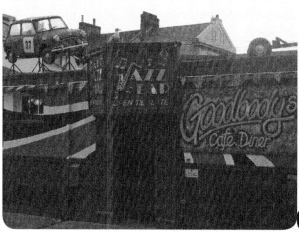

Flora and Fauna

Plymouth's waterfront lies on Devonian limestone and is nationally renowned for elements of its flora, including the Plymouth Thistle (*Carduus pycnocephalus*) and Plymouth Campion (*Silene vulgaris macrocarpa*).

Located at the mouth of the River Tamar, Devil's Point, in Stonehouse, not only offers stunning views across Plymouth Sound and over to Mount Edgcumbe but lies within the Plymouth Sound and Estuaries European Marine Site. The site hosts a vast underwater rock reef with overhangs, vertical cliff faces and submerged caves that extend to a depth of 30m. It is a favourite spot for anglers and divers, but beware the treacherous rip tides.

The area is of international conservation importance due to its wealth of marine and coastal wildlife. Rare species recorded at the site are the gold and scarlet star coral and the pink sea fan.

Born in Plymouth

John Hawkins, merchant adventurer and slave trader, 1532

Sir Joshua Reynolds, painter and first president of the Royal Academy, 1723

Eliza Parsons, gothic novelist, 1739

Sir George Arthur, 1st Baronet, Colonial Governor, 1784

Benjamin Robert Haydon, painter, 1786

Jonathan Nash Herder, electrical engineer, 1809

William Derry, wealthy benefactor and three-times Mayor of Plymouth, 1817

Louis Emanuel, composer, 1819

Sir James Robert Dickson, Australian politician and the thirteenth Premier of Queensland, 1832

Captain Robert Falcon Scott (Scott of the Antarctic), Antarctic explorer, 1868

Isaac Foot, politician and solicitor, 1880

Robert Victor Walling, soldier, journalist and poet, 1890

Michael Foot, politician, journalist and author, 1913

Sir Donald Sinden CBE, actor, 1923

Tony Soper, naturalist, wildlife cameraman and film producer, 1929

Angela Mortimer, former World No.1 British female tennis player, 1932

David Owen, politician, 1938

George Passmore, artist (best known as part of the duo Gilbert & George), 1942

Angela Rippon MBE, television journalist, newsreader and presenter, 1944

Maggie Steed, actress and comedienne, 1946

Bob Weston, musician and former member of Fleetwood Mac, 1947

Wayne Sleep OBE, dancer and choreographer, 1948

Trevor Francis, Britain's first £1m footballer player (when he joined Nottingham Forest in 1978), 1954

John Inverdale, radio and television broadcaster, mainly covering sporting events, 1957

Sharron Davies MBE, Olympic swimmer, 1962

Will James, Wales International Rugby Union player, 1976

Kate Nesbitt, first woman in the Royal Navy to be awarded the Military Cross, 1988

Lee Bridgman, dancer and finalist in 2011's *So You Think You Can Dance?*, 1990

Tom Daley, Olympic diver, 1994

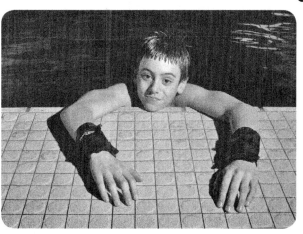

Died in Plymouth

Captain Andrew Henry, recipient of the Victoria Cross, Ford Park Cemetery, 1870

Lieutenant General John Campbell, Waterloo veteran, Ford Park Cemetery, 1871

Reverend Robert Stephen Hawker, Anglican priest and writer, Ford Park Cemetery, 1875

Jonathan Nash Hearder, engineer and inventor, Ford Park Cemetery, 1876

Dr John Butter, founder of the Royal Eye Infirmary, Ford Park Cemetery, 1877

Michael Keating (aka Tristram Shandy), cartoonist, ventriloquist, conjuror and manager of St James's Hall in Union Street, Ford Park Cemetery, 1895

George Hinkley, recipient of the Victoria Cross, Ford Park Cemetery, 1904

Peter Grillage, a Russian orphan whom Florence Nightingale brought back from the Crimea. He later became a butler at Chaddlewood House, Plympton, Ford Park Cemetery, 1907

Commander John Neil Robertson, inventor of the Neil Robertson folding stretcher, Ford Park Cemetery, 1914

Robert Lenkiewicz, painter, buried according to his wishes in the garden of his home at Lower Compton, 2002

Beryl Cook, painter, 2008

ROBERT STEPHEN
HAWKER
1804 — 1875
ECCENTRIC PARSON POET OF
MORWENSTOW WAS BORN HERE.
ORIGINATOR OF THE HARVEST
FESTIVAL SERVICE AND AUTHOR OF
THE LINES OF THE FAMOUS CORNISH
SONG ..."AND SHALL TRELAWNEY
DIE THERE'S 20,000 CORNISHMEN
WILL KNOW THE
REASON WHY"

Crimes and Criminals

Over 140 French prisoners of war were executed at the Hangmen's Cell at Plymouth's naval dockyard during the Napoleonic Wars.

John Barnes was fined 30s for Sabbath-breaking and set one hour in the stocks in the early 1600s.

Three Royal Marines were executed on Plymouth Hoe by firing squad in July 1797 for 'mutiny and sedition'.

Born in Plymouth in 1921, Merchant Seaman Duncan Scott-Ford was hanged by Albert Pierrepoint at Wandsworth Prison on 3 November 1942 for treachery, after supplying information to an enemy agent during the Second World War. He was twenty-one years old.

James Bilson was hanged at Gallows Cross, Heavitree, Exeter, on 6 April 1801 for the theft of seventeen seamen's beds and nineteen hammocks from the Naval Stores at Plymouth.

William Smith was hanged at Gallows Cross, Heavitree, Exeter, on 9 April 1802, for stealing a piece of muslin, twelve shawls and three lengths of silk at East Stonehouse, Plymouth.

James Hughes was hanged at Gallows Cross, Heavitree, Exeter, on 9 April 1802, for passing forged £5 notes at Plymouth.

Thirty-two-year-old Betsy Hulee was hanged at Exeter Gaol on 12 August 1805 for murdering her husband, William Rogers, at Plymouth. The *Exeter Flying Post* reported: 'On Monday last Betsy Hulee was executed at the drop, over the county gaol, and her body was delivered to the surgeons for dissection, pursuant to her sentence. From the moment of her conviction, to that of being launched into eternity, she conducted herself with Christian penitence becoming her unhappy situation.'

Ghosts

The Elizabethan House, the Barbican
Visitors to this restored Tudor sea captain's dwelling have seen a child's cradle rocking from side to side by itself, a young girl sitting in a corner of the first-floor room and seen looking out of the window from the street, and heard the sound of furniture being dragged around on floors above, when no one is up there.

Black Friars Distillery, Southside Street
Once a Dominican Order monastery, built in 1431, the distillery is said to be home to a ghostly monk who continues to roam the ancient passageways.

Her Majesty's Naval Base, Devonport
The ghost of a young girl has been seen playing in the Master Ropemaker's House, and paranormal activity reported in the Hangman's Cell, where over 140 French prisoners of war were executed.

Clifton Place, North Hill
An exorcism was held on 1 June 1964 after poltergeist activity was reported at a residential flat. The family living there witnessed coal flying around the room and glass tumblers being moved by unseen hands.

Albertha Ward, Greenbank Hospital (no longer standing)
The shade of Lady Albertha, who donated money for a ward to be built at the hospital, used to appear beside the cots of sick children. When she appeared, the child was sure to recover, regardless of how ill they were.

The Hairy Hands of Dartmoor
Although not technically in Plymouth, the legendary 'Hairy Hands of Dartmoor' have terrorized drivers and motorcyclists on the B3212 between Postbridge and Two Bridges since around 1910. In many cases, the victims reported that the vehicle had been forcibly steered off the side of the road, as if something had taken hold of the wheel and wrenched it out of their control.

THIS EARLY
15TH CENTURY
BUILDING
FORMED PART OF THE
MONASTERY
OF THE
DOMINICANS
OR
"BLACKFRIARS"

Favourite Scene

Least Favourite Scene

Colourful Characters

Robert Lenkiewicz

Robert Lenkiewicz (1941–2002) was one of the South
West's most talented artists and regarded by many as one
of the most gifted figurative painters of modern times.
Lenkiewicz moved to Plymouth in about 1969 after being
offered studio space on the Barbican by local artist John
Nash. Recognisable around the Barbican by his long hair and
beard, Lenkiewicz's impoverished life mirrored that of his
sitters, who included many vagrants. He first came to public
attention when the media highlighted his giant mural on
the Barbican in the 1970s, one of several large-scale public
murals he painted there.

Beryl Cook OBE

Beryl Cook (1926–2008) began to paint in her late forties
and quickly found success with her colourful, flamboyant
characters inspired by Plymouth's pub life. Along with all
the tourists, sailors and Plymothians she saw by day, Beryl
particularly enjoyed watching Plymouth come alive at night,
and the Dolphin pub on the Barbican in particular provided
many fun-loving, larger-than-life characters for Beryl's
paintings.

Jack the Plymouth Town Crier

Jack, real name David Saunders, grew up in Plymouth and
as well as being the city's lively Town Crier – appearing
at events, promotions and street advertising for retailers
and product launches – is also a professional MC and runs
'Plymouth Buzz', an internet newspaper full of positive
things about Plymouth (www.plymouthbuzz.com)

Local Lingo

'Janners' – People born in Plymouth

'Reet?' – Alright?

'Alreet me lover?' – How are you, my dear?

'Mitching' – Playing truant

'Cakey' – Childish/girlish

'Where's it to?' – Where is it?

'Bay' – Boy

Commemorative Plaques

Admiral Hardy (1769–1839), captain of the fleet at Trafalgar and witness to Nelson's immortal dying words aboard HMS *Victory*, 'Kismet Hardy'.

156 Durnford Street, Stonehouse

Sir Francis Drake (1540–1596), English sea captain.

Corner shop, Looe Street

Lt J.R.M. Chard (1847–1897), hero of the defence of Rorke's Drift by 104 men against the onslaught of 4,000 Zulu warriors on 22 January 1879.

Kitto Sports Centre

William Friese Green (1855–1921), early pioneer of cinematography who opened a photographic shop and studio in Plymouth in 1880.

Two Trees pub, Union Street

Lawrence of Arabia (1883–1935). On his return from India in 1929, T.E. Lawrence, under the assumed name of Shaw, was posted to a flying boat squadron at RAF Mount Batten.

St John's Road, Plymstock

Captain R.F. Scott, 'Scott of the Antarctic' (1868–1912), explorer.

Outland Road

Alexander Selkirk (1676–1721), Scottish sailor marooned on Juan Fernandez Island in 1704, his story became the basis of Daniel Defoe's book *Robinson Crusoe*.

Marine Road, Plymstock

John Smeaton (1721–1792), civil engineer.

Smeaton's Tower, Plymouth Hoe

Captain James Cook (1728–1779), captain in the Royal Navy and leader of three voyages of discovery which chartered unknown land in the South Seas and Pacific. On each voyage he set out from Plymouth.

Notte Street, the Barbican

HERE
REPUTEDLY LIVED
ADMIRAL SIR T.M.HARDY
BART. G.C.B., BORN 1769
CAPTAIN OF THE FLEET
AT TRAFALGAR 1805
AND WITNESS TO NELSON'S
IMMORTAL DYING WORDS
ABOARD H.M.S. VICTORY
'KISS ME HARDY'
FIRST SEA LORD 1830-1834
GOVERNOR
GREENWICH HOSPITAL
1834
DIED 1839

SIR
FRANCIS DRAKE,
IN THE YEAR
OF THE
∘ SPANISH ARMADA, ∘
OWNED A HOUSE AND
GROUNDS UPON THIS
SITE, AND PROBABLY
HERE
RESIDED.

The Barbican Then & Now

Festivals and Events

The Barbican International Jazz & Blues Festival,
April-May

www.barbicanjazzandbluesfestival.com

Plymouth Half Marathon, May

www.plymouthhalfmarathon.co.uk

Pirate Days Plymouth, May

www.piratedaysplymouth.com

Plymouth Summer Festival, May-September

www.plymouthsummerfestival.com

Plymouth Volksfest, June

www.plymouthvolksfest.co.uk

Race for Life Plymouth, June

www.raceforlife.org

CAMRA Plymouth Beer Festival, July

www.camra.org.uk

Port of Plymouth Regatta, July-August

www.plymouthregatta.com

Love Parks Week, July

www.plymouth.gov.uk

British Firework Championships, August
www.britishfireworks.co.uk

The Plymouth Air Show, August
www.plymouthairshow.co.uk

Mount Edgcumbe Classic Car Show, August
www.plymouth.gov.uk/meevents

Flavour Fest, August
www.plymouth.gov.uk/flavourfest

The America's Cup World Series (the world's oldest sporting trophy), September 2011
www.americascup.com

Navy Days, September (biannual)
www.navydaysuk.co.uk

Plymouth Respect Festival, October
www.plymouthrespectfestival.co.uk

Plymouth Winter Festival, November-December
www.plymouthwinterfestival.com

Highly Recommended

Elizabethan Gardens, New Street, the Barbican
Leading off New Street is this walled garden, planted with old plant varieties to recreate an authentic Elizabethan garden. The garden is free to enter and offers a tranquil atmosphere in the heart of the busy Barbican.

The Seven Stars Inn, Tamerton Foliot, Plymouth
The monks of Plympton Priory are believed to have used this building as a hostelry in the fourteenth century, thus making the Seven Stars a candidate for being the oldest pub in modern Plymouth.

Tanners Restaurant, Prysten House, Finewell Street
Opened in 1999 by celebrity TV chefs Chris and James Tanner, the restaurant is housed in the oldest surviving domestic building in Plymouth, Prysten House. With its combination of rich medieval history and modern menu, it is a popular eatery.

Worth's Bone Caves, Cattedown
First discovered in 1886, the Bone Caves are part of a huge system of caverns thought to spread beneath the length and breadth of Cattedown and to around 50m below sea level. Local naturalist R.N. Worth and his colleagues discovered the remains of at least fifteen hominids, and the 'Cattedown Man' bones are believed to be up to 140,000 years old.

Plymouth Arts Centre, 38 Looe Street
Plymouth Arts Centre features local and international contemporary art exhibitions, an independent cinema programme, and a thriving café bar.

Parade Antiques and Curios Museum, the Barbican
This seventeenth-century warehouse houses over sixty display cabinets containing artwork, china, glass and ceramics, antique furniture, jewellery, coins and medals, toys, film and TV memorabilia. It also houses such items as Charlie Chaplin's first tramp suit, a full-size Dalek and a Cyberman from *Doctor Who*.

University of Plymouth Honorary Degrees

Matthew Bellamy, Dominic Howard and Christopher Wolstenholme of the Devon rock band Muse received Honorary Doctorates of Arts from the university in 2008. 'I'm pretty sure we're not worthy,' said frontman Matt Bellamy when the band joined students to collect the prize.

Pam St Clement, the *EastEnders* star, received an Honorary Doctorate of Education in 2008. The actress grew up in Devon and qualified as a teacher at Rolle Teacher Training College in Exmouth (now part of the University of Plymouth). She worked in education until joining the cast in Albert Square, playing the role of Pat Evans in the soap between 1986 and 2012.

Seth Lakeman, the Dartmoor-born award-winning singer-songwriter, received an Honorary Doctorate of Music in 2009.

Sir Trevor McDonald OBE, the ITV legend received an Honorary Doctorate of Letters from the university in 1993.

Alastair Stewart, ITV news presenter and journalist, was presented with an Honorary Doctorate of Letters in 2010.

Dick Strawbridge MBE, presenter of *Scrapheap Challenge* and finalist in *Celebrity MasterChef* 2010, received an Honorary Doctorate of Science in 2010. Dick runs eco courses from his farm in Cornwall.

Sir Ranulph Fiennes OBE, the first man to reach both poles by land and the oldest Briton to climb Everest, received an Honorary Doctorate of Science in 2011.

Phillip Schofield, television presenter who grew up in Newquay, Cornwall, returned to the South West in 2011 to receive an Honorary Doctorate of Arts in recognition of his stage and television career.

Chris Hines MBE, founder of SurfersAgainst Sewage and former Director of Sustainability at the Eden Project, was awarded an Honorary Doctorate of Science in 2011.

Sports Teams

Plymouth Raiders

Officially called UCP Marjon Plymouth Raiders for sponsorship reasons, the Plymouth Raiders are the South West's leading basketball team. They play their home games at the Plymouth Pavilions Arena and have competed in the top tier of British Basketball League since 2004.

Plymouth Devils

The speedway team was re-formed in 2006 after a gap of thirty-six years by former St Austell Gulls rider Mike Bowden. The Devils' home track today is the 260m St Boniface Arena.

Plymouth Albion Rugby Football Club

Founded in about 1915 from a merger between Plymouth RFC and Devonport Albion RFC, Plymouth Albion were a major force in English rugby union in the 1920s. They were promoted to National Division One in 2002, and finished third in the 2003/4 season. The team went on a two-season unbeaten streak of over fifty games, starting when the club was in Division Three South and ending after their promotion to National Division One. Albion play their home games at Brickfields Recreation Ground.

Plymouth Argyle Football Club

The club was formed in September 1886. Argyle's first home venue was at Freedom Fields. Today, the NPower League Two club play their home games at Home Park, a £50m stadium with a capacity of 18,000. Since turning professional in 1903, the club has won five Football League titles and one Western League title. However, Plymouth Argyle has never played at the top level of English football, coming closest in 1953 when they finished fourth in the old Second Division. The club takes its nickname 'The Pilgrims' from the Pilgrim Fathers who sailed from Plymouth for the New World in 1620, and the club's crest features their ship, the *Mayflower*. The team's official mascot is Pilgrim Pete. Despite the club celebrating 125 years since the founding of Plymouth Argyle in 2011, the club went into administration in the same year with debts of almost £18m.

A-Z

A

Argyle: since becoming professional in 1903, Plymouth Argyle Football Club has won five Football League titles, five Southern League titles and one Western League title. They are the most southern and western League club in England.

B

Big Screen: installed in 2008 in Plymouth city centre ahead of the Beijing Olympics, it is one of twenty BBC Big Screens located in cities across the UK. Measuring 25sq.m, it is a focal point for the city's open-air entertainment, showing a wide range of broadcasts including sporting events, opera and Hollywood blockbusters.

C

Cap'n Jaspers: this open-air café on the Barbican has been feeding hungry locals and visitors for over thirty years. Favourites on the menu include the Jasperizer and the Cap'n Special. The small building was formerly manned by three regular policemen, who kept a stove and a supply of grappling irons for retrieving bodies from the harbour.

D

Drake, Sir Francis: English sea captain, pirate, hero and Lord Mayor of Plymouth between 1581 and 1582. Legend has it that Drake was playing bowls on Plymouth Hoe when told that the Spanish Armada had arrived. He coolly declared that there was time to finish the match and then defeat the Spanish; he lost the game, but won the battle.

E

Edgcumbe: Mount Edgcumbe House was first built in the 1500s and is the former home of the Earls of Mount Edgcumbe. It is set within 865 acres of parkland on the Rame Peninsula, Cornwall, and is jointly owned by Cornwall County Council and Plymouth City Council.

F

Fishing: the most important industry in Tudor Plymouth, for centuries the Barbican was home to Plymouth's fish market and is still home to many fishermen.

G

Gin: Black Friars Distillery on Southside Street has been the working home of Plymouth Gin since 1793, making it the oldest working gin distillery in England.

H

Harry Houdini: Houdini appeared at the Palace Theatre of Varieties, Union Street, in August 1909.

I

Ivor Dewdney: the company has been in business since the 1930s, when Ivor opened his first shop in King Street, Plymouth. Theirs was voted 'Best Pasty' by the people of Plymouth in 2002. Today, the company offers a new service – 'Pasties by Post'. (www.ivordewdney.co.uk)

J

Jazz and Blues Festival: started in 2008, the festival features local and international acts performing gigs at various locations across the city.

K

Kingdom Brunel, Isambard: designed the Royal Albert Bridge (opened by His Royal Highness Prince Albert in May 1859), taking the railway over the River Tamar from Devon into Cornwall.

L

Leat: known variably as Drake's Leat and Plymouth Leat, this watercourse was constructed in the late sixteenth century to tap the River Meavy on Dartmoor in order to supply Plymouth with water.

M

Mount Batten: this 24m-tall outcrop of rock is set on a 600m peninsula in Plymouth Sound.

N

Naval Base: HMNB Devonport is the largest naval base in Western Europe. It covers 650 acres and has fifteen dry docks, twenty-five tidal berths and five basins. There are 5,000 ship movements annually and it is estimated that the base generates about 10 per cent of the income for Plymouth.

O

Olympians: Tom Daley represented Great Britain at the 2008 Summer Olympics, where he was Britain's youngest competitor. He won two gold medals at the 2010 Commonwealth Games in the 10m synchro diving and the 10m individual platform competition, and will be competing at the 2012 Olympic Games in London. Swimmer Sharron Davies won a silver medal in the 400m individual medley at the 1980 Olympics in Mosow, and two gold medals at the 1978 Commonwealth Games in Edmonton.

P

Pilgrim Fathers: after setting sail in the *Mayflower* from Plymouth in 1620, the Pilgrim Fathers founded the first permanent European settlement in New England – the Plymouth Colony (present-day Plymouth, Massachusetts, USA).

Q

Queen Anne's Battery: this marina has 235 permanent berths for boats up to 18m. QAB is also home to the Royal Western Yacht Club, and many international short-handed yacht races start and finish here, including the single-handed Transatlantic Race, the Round Britain Race and the Rolex Fastnet Race.

R

River Tamar: forms the border between Devon and Cornwall. It is spanned by the Royal Albert Bridge (railway) and Tamar Bridge (toll road) between Plymouth and Saltash.

S

Sundial: a popular meeting point in the heart of the city centre. At 27ft tall, it was designed by architect Carole Vincent and was unveiled by Her Majesty the Queen in 1988, at a cost of £70,000.

T

Tinside Lido: this art deco open-air swimming pool was built in 1935. Situated on Plymouh Hoe, it is open between May and September. Sunloungers and deckchairs are available for hire.

U

University of Plymouth: the university has a student population of approximately 30,000. The university's motto is *Indagate Fingite Invenite*, meaning 'Explore, Dream, Discover'.

V

Victoria Park: the park was formally opened to the public in 1903. The park had three air-raid shelters to protect the population during the Blitz.

W

Wheel of Plymouth: situated on the Hoe, this 60m-tall wheel – twice as high as Smeaton's Tower – offers 360-degree views of the city and Plymouth Sound. With forty-two enclosed capsules, the ride lasts approximately thirteen minutes.

X

X80: First Devon and Cornwall's bus service between Plymouth and Torquay.

Y

Yacht Operations: this FdSc course is offered by the University of Plymouth in conjunction with South Devon College.

Z

Zoo: formerly located in Central Park, Plymouth Zoo opened in April 1962 and closed in January 1978. It was home to around 200 animals, including tigers, giraffes, elephants and sea lions.

Laurel and Hardy

Comedy double act and Hollywood stars Laurel and Hardy appeared at the Palace Theatre, Union Street, on Monday, 17 May 1954. Stan and Ollie were touring the country in a comedy entitled *Birds of a Feather*. Playing on the same bill were 'Betty Kaye's Pekinese Pets' and 'Wonder Horse Tony'. Unfortunately, whilst in Plymouth, Hardy reportedly suffered a mild heart attack and so the duo decided to cancel the rest of their UK stage tour and return home to the US. The *New York Times* reported on 21 May 1954:

OLIVER HARDY SLIGHTLY IMPROVED

PLYMOUTH, England — Physicians reported a slight improvement today in the condition of Oliver Hardy, American film comedian, who is ill with pneumonia. Mr. Hardy, partner of Stan Laurel in the famous screen comedy team, had to discontinue an engagement at a Plymouth theatre. He plans to return to the United States as soon as he is able to travel.

Ollie spent the remainder of his stay recovering at the Grand Hotel on Plymouth Hoe, after which the slapstick comedians returned to America – sailing from Hull aboard the MS *Manchuria* on 2 June.

Oliver Hardy died of a stroke in August 1957. Stan Laurel died in February 1965.

PALACE THEATRE

PLYMOUTH

Managing Director: GERARD HEATH   General Manager: Wm. WILLIS

Advance Bookings Phone: PLYMOUTH 4383 and 5347   BOX OFFICE OPEN 10 a.m. to 8 p.m.

6-20 ★ MONDAY, MAY 17th
Mat.: SATURDAY 2.30 ★ **8.35**

HOLLYWOOD'S GREATEST COMEDY COUPLE!

HERE IN PERSON

STAN   BERNARD DELFONT *presents*   OLIVER

LAUREL AND HARDY

IN A NEW COMEDY "BIRDS OF A FEATHER"

DEREK ROSAIRE *presents his*	PEGGY CAVELL THE CARTOON GIRL	HARRY WORTH	DOROTHY REID & MACK SCOTTISH ACE ACCORDIONISTS	
WONDER HORSE TONY	ALAN ROWE BORN TO IMPRESS	FIGURE OF SPEECH MARY & MICHAEL MILLS	TRIO BOTANDO Sensational Balancers	BETTY KAYE'S PEKINESE PETS

TRIBE BROS., Ltd., London & St. Albans

Great Liners

The 1920s and '30s were the golden age of the transatlantic liners and many renowned ships, including *Queen Mary*, *Mauretania* (the world's fastest liner from 1907–27) and *Normandie* (which arrived in Plymouth Sound in 1937 after crossing the Atlantic in record-breaking time), all called at Plymouth, disembarking mail and passengers who then transferred to trains from Millbay Docks for London and Southampton. To the delight of Plymothians, who would line the docks, famous stars including Gloria Swanson, Jack Warner, Mary Pickford, Rudolph Valentino, Bing Crosby and Walt Disney were often among the passengers. Charlie Chaplin, who disembarked from *Mauretania* in 1931, was the guest of Nancy Astor at her home in Elliott Terrace on the Hoe.

From the 1870s, visiting mail and passenger steamers anchored in the Sound rather than docking at Millbay, and a fleet of tenders transported passengers and mail to and from the docks. Over six million passengers were landed or embarked from Millbay during the twentieth century with liner traffic peaking in the 1930s (788 liners called at Plymouth in 1930) and declining after the Second World War.

Two Maritime Disasters

Millbay Docks received survivors from two of the world's greatest maritime disasters – one a peacetime accident, the other a wartime tragedy:

Titanic

On 14 April 1912, the White Star liner *Titanic* sank on her maiden voyage from Southampton to New York after hitting an iceberg, with the loss of about 1,500 lives. On Sunday, 28 April 1912, thirteen days after the tragedy, the Red Star liner SS *Lapland* brought 167 surviving crewmembers who had been detained in America for the US inquiry into Plymouth, mooring at Cawsand Bay, with the tender *Sir Richard Grenville* eventually landing them at Millbay Docks. The crew was put on a special train from here to Southampton.

Lancastria

On 17 June 1940, the Cunard liner *Lancastria*, serving as a troopship during the Second World War, was sunk during an attack by German Junkers 88 aircraft whilst helping to evacuate British military forces from the French port of St Nazaire, with an estimated loss of at least 4,000 lives. On arrival at Plymouth, rescue vessels brought the survivors into Millbay Docks. Volunteers gave out tea, food and writing materials, while civilians and shop owners organised free fish and chips, and cigarettes. The injured were taken to local hospitals and others were sent to billets – including Stonehouse Barracks, the Naval Barracks, RAF Mount Batten, the Ballard Institute and local church halls – to get washed and re-clothed.

War Memorials

National Armada Memorial, Plymouth Hoe
Commemorating the defeat of the Spanish Armada, 1588.

Sabbath Day Fight Memorial, Freedom Fields Park
English Civil War battlesite, 1643.

South African War Memorial, Plymouth Hoe
Remembrance of those killed in the Boer War.

Doris Gun, Devonport Park
Remembrance of those killed on HMS *Doris* during the Boer War.

Burma Star, Plymouth Hoe
Remembrance of those killed in Burma.

Civilian Memorial, Efford Cemetary
Remembering those that perished during the Plymouth Blitz in 1941.

Normandy Landings Monument, Saltash Passage
Commemorating those Americans who sailed from Plymouth for Normandy in 1944.

Regent Brewery Great War Memorial, Durnford Street
Remembrance of those killed in the First World War.

Laira Great War Memorial, Old Laira Road
Remembrance of those killed in the First World War.

War Memorial, Alexandra Park
Remembering those who lost their lives in the Second World War.

Royal Australian Air Force Memorial, Sutton Harbour
Remembering those who served with 10 Squadron in the Second World War.

Remembrance of those killed in the two world wars:

Royal Marine Memorial, Plymouth Hoe
Royal Air Force and Allied Air Forces Monument, Plymouth Hoe
Plymouth War Memorial, Plymouth Hoe
Plymouth Naval War Memorial, Plymouth Hoe
War Memorial, Devonport Park
War Memorial, Tamerton Foliot
War Memorial, Plympton Castle
War Memorial, Burrow Hill, Plymstock
Cross of Sacrifice, Ford Park Cemetery

Other conflicts:

Korean Veterans, Plymouth Hoe
Remembrance of those killed in Korea

Falklands War Memorial, Plymouth Hoe
Remembrance of those killed in the Falklands

Commando Gunner Memorial, Royal Citadel
Memorial to personnel killed while serving with
29 Commando Regiment Royal Artillery

Statues, Sculptures and Art Installations

Aquatic Circus installation by Jan Blake, Drake Circus shopping centre

Ten brightly coloured tensile silk fish structures are suspended in the semi-circular atrium space. Each fish is suspended by one point, allowing it to turn slowly and interact with a neighbouring fish.

The 'Barbican Prawn', the Barbican

This sculpture represents varieties of fish and other marine life landed on the Barbican.

Britannia by W. Charles May, Plymouth Hoe, bronze

Standing atop the National Armada Memorial on Plymouth Hoe, she stands 11ft 6in tall and bears a trident, sword and shield. The memorial was unveiled in 1890.

Riding a Wave by Lucy Glendinning, Drake Circus shopping centre, stainless steel base and lacquered aluminium figure

Installed in October 2006 to commemorate the opening of the new Drake Circus shopping centre in the heart of Plymouth city centre, the figure is hanging onto the top as if holding onto the wave. This piece responds to the architecture as if coming out of the corner of the glass building.

Sir Francis Drake by Joseph Boehm, Plymouth Hoe, bronze

This statue is located on the Hoe, where Francis Drake was playing bowls when the Spanish Armada approached England. Beside him is a bronze globe, representing his successful circumnavigation of the world between 1577 and 1580.

Totem Pole carved by Lee Dickenson, North Cross roundabout, cedar

This 18ft pole depicts the animals found by Charles Darwin on his trip to the Galapagos Islands. In 1831 Darwin sailed from Plymouth aboard the *Beagle* for the Galapagos Islands, where he formulated his revolutionary theories of natural selection.

The Unknown Airman by Pamela Taylor, Plymouth Hoe, bronze

Unveiled by Air Marshal Sir John Curtiss on Sunday, 3 September 1989, the 6ft-tall statue stands atop the granite Royal Air Force and Allied Air Forces Monument.

King Billy's statue, Mutton Cove, fibreglass

The statue that stands beside the dockyard at Mutton Cove, known as King Billy, is of William IV and was originally a figurehead on the 120-gun warship *Royal William*. In the 1990s, the wooden figurehead was deteriorating fast so it was decided to make a fibreglass copy, which now stands in place of the original, which has now been restored and stands alongside other preserved figureheads at Black Yarn Stores at Devonport Dockyard.

King William IV by Sir John Rennie, Royal William Victualling Yard, Portland stone

The Royal William Victualling Yard is named after King William IV, the last Lord High Admiral. Above the granite entrance gateway in Cremyll Street is Rennie's 13ft 9in-high statue of the king, surrounded by carvings illustrating the trades that flourished inside the walls: butchers, bakers and coopers.

The Scott Memorial, Mount Wise, bronze

Captain Robert Falcon Scott was born at Milehouse, Plymouth, on 6 June 1868. On 1 November 1911, Scott set out on a doomed race to be the first to reach the South Pole, reaching it in January 1912 – a month behind his Norwegian rival, Amundsen. Captain Scott and his five-man team died in March 1912 on the return journey, 11 miles short of a supply depot.

HMS *Ark Royal* anchor, junction of Aramada Way & Notte Street

This Royal Naval aircraft carrier was a Devonport-based ship and underwent several re-fits at the dockyard in Plymouth. On 4 December 1978 she entered the dockyard for the last time and was decommissioned on 14 February 1979. On 24 April 1980, Lord Hill-Norton, Admiral of the Fleet, presented one of the anchors to the city of Plymouth and it was unveiled in the presence of the Lord Mayor Graham Jinks and Mrs Ted Anson, the wife of *Ark Royal*'s last commanding officer.

Little-Known Facts

Belisha beacons are named after Leslie Hore-Belisha, who was born in Devonport in 1893 and was appointed Minister of Transport in 1934. He added beacons to pedestrian crossings marked by large metal studs in the road surface. These crossings were later painted in black and white stripes and are today known as zebra crossings.

Catherine of Aragon arrived in Plymouth from Spain in 1501, on her way to marry Prince Arthur at St Paul's Cathedral. She later famously became Henry VIII's first wife, in 1509.

In 1919 Nancy Astor became the first woman Member of Parliament, representing the constituency of Sutton in Plymouth. She is allegedly reported to have said to Winston Churchill on his visit to the blitzed city in May 1941, 'If you were my husband, I'd put arsenic in your coffee,' to which he retorted, 'Madame, if I were your husband, I'd drink it!'

In 1768 William Cookworthy discovered the process for making porcelain using clay from a Cornish quarry and subsequently set up a factory in Plymouth – The China House, which is today a pub and restaurant on Sutton Wharf.

The first burial at Ford Park Cemetery took place in December 1848.

Plymouth's first Boy Scout troop was registered with scouting headquarters in London on 4 July 1908, the year that the movement was founded. It was allied to All Saints' Church in Harwell Street.

In 1787, two convict ships, *Friendship* and *Charlotte*, sailed from Plymouth for Australia.

Sir Francis Chichester left Plymouth on 27 August 1966 in his ketch *Gipsy Moth IV* and circumnavigated the world single-handed, arriving back in Plymouth on 28 May 1967 after 266 days.

The Rolling Stones played at the former ABC cinema in Plymouth on 27 August 1964 – the only time they played in the city.

What's in a Name?

Plymouth has been a naval port for hundreds of years, so it is no surprise that many of its shops, businesses, streets and thoroughfares are named after key historical events and people that have shaped the city's maritime history.

Telegraph Wharf recalls the loading of 3,000 miles of cable onto two naval vessels – the British *Agamemnon* and the American *Niagara* – at Keyham Yard, which was to span the Atlantic. The first transatlantic message was received in County Kerry, Ireland from Trinity Bay, Newfoundland, in 1858.

Admiralty Street and Admiralty Road in Stonehouse both reflect the city's strong connection with the Royal Navy.

Elsewhere in the city, there are twenty-two businesses and one school called 'Drake', including Drake Hotel in Lockyer Street, Drake Dry Cleaning in Devonport's Albert Road, and Drake Primary School in Keyham.

There are seventeen businesses – including two schools and one college – called 'Mayflower', including Mayflower Carpet Cleaning Co. in St Budeaux, Mayflower Van Hire, the Mayflower Sailing Club at Phoenix Wharf, and Mayflower Street Launderette in, you've guessed it, Mayflower Street.

There are twelve businesses called 'Armada', including Armada Sports on Transit Way, Armada Florists in Cornwall Street, and the Armada shopping centre in, yep, Armada Way.

There are six businesses and one school called 'Pilgrim', including Pilgrim Pasties and Pilgrim Primary School.

Local pubs recall the city's seafaring and industrial heritage, including the Devonport Inn, the Fisherman's Arms, the Eddystone Inn, the Artillery Arms, the Maritime Inn, the Two Bridges Inn, the Navy Inn, and the Royal Albert Bridge Inn, among others.

Websites

www.plymouth.gov.uk

www.thisisplymouth.co.uk

www.visitplymouth.co.uk

www.plymouthu3a.co.uk (University of the Third Age)

www.plymouth.ac.uk (University of Plymouth)

www.plymouthgin.com

www.pafc.co.uk (Plymouth Argyle Football Club)

www.plymouthalbion.com (Plymouth Albion Rugby Club)

www.plymouthmuseum.gov.uk

www.upsu.com (University of Plymouth Students' Union)

www.plymouthmag.com

www.facebook.com/pages/Plymouth/107666599263369

twitter.com/plymouth_devon

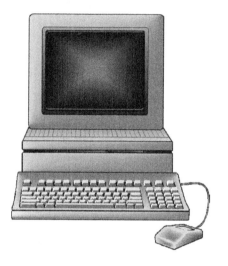

Advertisements from Yesteryear

SHIPPING SUPPLIED

WITH

LIVE & DEAD

STOCK.

TELEPHONE N⁰. 114.

JOHN SHILLABEER,

PURVEYOR,

15, THE MARKET,

PLYMOUTH.

PRIVATE FAMILES WAITED ON DAILY.   DISTANCE NO OBJECT.

PLIMSAUL BROS.

41, BEDFORD STREET,

9 & 10 East Street, & 8 & 9 Week Street.

Reversible Hood 33/-
33/-

Resnic Car 30/-
30/-

A LARGE VARIETY OF

PERAMBULATORS AND BASSINETTES

TO CHOOSE FROM.   BASSINETTE PERAMBULATORS from 30/- each.

SOLE AGENTS FOR THE NEW HAMMOCK PERAMBULATOR.

Write for Illustrated Catalogue. ÷ Carriage Paid on Orders over £2 Nett to any Railway Station,

TEN PER CENT DISCOUNT FOR CASH WITH ORDER.

Registered Telegraphic Address— PLIMBROS, PLYMOUTH.   TELEPHONE No. 105.

The Plymouth Blitz

On 20 March 1941, King George VI and Queen Elizabeth arrived in Plymouth for a tour of the dockyard and an inspection of the Civil Defence and Voluntary Services in Guildhall Square. They were chaperoned by and later took tea with Lord and Lady Astor. They left the city at 5.30 p.m. on the royal train, less than three hours before some 125 enemy aircraft bombed the city in a devastating raid that left 336 people dead and was to become known as the 'Plymouth Blitz'.

Overnight, Plymouth – a prime target due to the dockyard and its status as a major port – became the most heavily blitzed city in Britain. The city centre was devastated and around 18,000 buildings were damaged – including the pier.

St Andrew's Church was badly damaged. However, amidst the smoking ruins a headmistress nailed over the door a wooden sign which read *Resurgam* (Latin for 'I shall rise again'), indicating the wartime spirit. A carved granite plaque inscribed with the word is now permanently fixed above the church's entrance.

Charles Cross was destroyed by incendiaries, but was preserved in its ruined state as a memorial to civilian victims of the Blitz.

Streets and schools were hit, including Plymouth High School for Girls, the Hoe Grammar School and the infants' school at Summerland Place. Many churches were also destroyed, including St James the Less, King Street Methodist, St Peter's and George Street Baptist among others. The Guildhall on Royal Parade survived the bombing raids.

Further raids over the next four weeks brought the death toll in Plymouth to 926. During an attack by the Luftwaffe on the evening of 22 April 1941, a communal air-raid shelter at Portland Square took a direct hit, killing seventy-two people. The University of Plymouth has named a building on its site after the tragedy.

Prime Minister Winston Churchill visited the city on 2 May 1941 and toured the blitzed areas.

The Plan for Plymouth

Professor Patrick Abercrombie drew up the 'Plan for Plymouth' in 1943 after the city was heavily bombed during the Second World War. Large areas had been flattened, including the city centre, central Devonport and parts of Stonehouse. The 'Plan' was a revolutionary vision to create a new, modern city.

Rebuilding work began in 1947 and extended the city into Tamerton and Roborough, Plympton and Plymsock. The first kerbstone of the new city centre was laid on the edging of Derry's Cross roundabout on 17 March 1947, almost six years to the day since the Luftwaffe almost destroyed the city on 20 March 1941.

Along with new housing, improvements were made to the road network, along with the construction of new bridges, schools, shops and factories, which brought jobs to the city.

Freak Weather

21 August 1948
Heavy rain and winds reaching gale force lashed the West Country. Plymouth recorded almost an inch of rain at Mount Batten in only a few hours. Sutton Harbour Regatta had to be postponed, while at St Budeaux the Conservative fête had to move into a schoolroom.

1956
Plymouth headed the sunshine table this year, according to Air Ministry records collected weekly from twenty places in England, Wales and Northern Ireland. The city recorded 1,752 hours of sunshine.

11 December 1957
A tornado swept across the Hamoaze and heavy rain caused flooding following a fierce gale the previous night. Over 300 buildings were damaged in the city and power failures were widespread. Train journeys and ferry crossings were delayed as high winds made travel too dangerous.

29 January 1961
Severe gales swept across the West Country. In two separate incidents, a man and a woman were both blown over and taken to Greenbank Hospital suffering from head injuries.

16 October 1987
BBC weatherman Michael Fish said it wasn't going to happen, but on 16 October 1987 one of the worst storms in living memory wreaked havoc across southern England. With wind speeds of up to 100mph, the Great Storm, as it became known, resulted in several local people being injured and many schools were closed as tiles were lifted off roofs and trees were uprooted.

Television and Films

TV series and dramas filmed in and around Plymouth:

Although normally set around the rugged cliffs of Cornwall, an episode of the ITV detective drama **Wycliffe** (1994–98), starring Jack Shepherd, was filmed in Plymouth.

In 2002 the BBC filmed Arthur Conan Doyle's most famous Sherlock Holmes novel, **The Hound of the Baskervilles**, on location on Dartmoor. Richard Roxburgh led a star-studded cast as Sherlock Holmes, opposite Ian Hart as Dr Watson, with Liza Tarbuck playing Mrs Barrymore, Richard E. Grant as Stapleton and John Nettles as Dr Mortimer. The detective and his sidekick travel from London to Dartmoor to unravel the mystery of a spectral hound.

Jane Austen's **Sense and Sensibility** was filmed at Saltram House in 1995. Directed by Ang Lee and with a screenplay by Emma Thompson, the film is based on Austen's 1811 novel of the same name. Saltram House is a magnificent eighteenth-century National Trust mansion surrounded by a landscaped park and features exquisite plasterwork ceilings, Chinese wallpaper and Joshua Reynolds paintings. Other scenes were filmed at Efford House and Flete Estate in Plymouth.

Hollywood director Steven Spielberg was on Dartmoor in August 2010 filming scenes for the epic adventure **War Horse**, based on the novel by Devon author Michael Morpurgo. The story centres on farm horse Joey, who is sent to France at the outbreak of the First World War.

Also filmed on Dartmoor, **We Bought a Zoo**, starring Matt Damon, follows the story of the Mee family's purchase of Dartmoor Zoo in 2006. The film's premier was shown in New York in December 2011.

In 2010, the National Trust's eighteenth-century Antony House, near Plymouth, was transformed into a fabulous, surreal setting for Tim Burton's film **Alice in Wonderland**, starring Johnny Depp, Anne Hathway and Helena Bonham Carter.

Arthur Conan Doyle

At his request, Arthur Conan Doyle (1859–1930) joined fellow University of Edinburgh student George Turnavine Budd's medical practice at 1 Durnford Street, East Stonehouse, Plymouth, in 1882. The partnership lasted just seven weeks and Conan Doyle left for Southsea, Portsmouth.

While in Plymouth, Conan Doyle would undoubtedly have read the *Western Morning News*, which is mentioned in his later literary work *The Hound of the Baskervilles* (1902), which is set at the fictional Baskerville Hall on nearby Dartmoor.

Budd's medical practice in Durnford Street and other neighbouring buildings were demolished in 1958. The land was used to site Renwick's Garage. Today, a luxury apartment block – Evolution Cove – occupies the site.

There exist a series of twenty-two plaques featuring quotes from Sherlock Holmes stories set within the pavement between Nos 85 and 125 Durnford Street. An additional plaque is mounted on the lower step at the entrance to No. 93 Durnford Street.

Conan Doyle was a staunch supporter of Spiritualism and returned to Plymouth in 1923 to give a lecture entitled 'The New Revelation'.

The plot thickens

...is quite a three-pipe problem.

Famous for...

Being by the sea

Plymouth Gin

Elizabethan seafarer Sir Francis Drake

Smeaton's Tower

Olympic diver Tom Daley

Isambard Kingdom Brunel (Royal Albert Bridge)

British Firework Championships

Naval Barracks

The Elizabethan House

Plymouth Argyle FC

Infamous for...

1950s Architecture

With more listed 1950s buildings than anywhere outside London, English Heritage described Plymouth – the only British city to have the whole of its centre completely rebuilt after it was heavily bombed during the Second World War – 'as representative of its time as Bath or York'. Simon Thurley, Chief Executive of English Heritage, said in 2011: 'It is a unique place... The buildings have really strong qualities ... They are recognised by historians as being amongst the best buildings built anywhere in the 1950s... if the owners of the buildings and the council took more pride in them the city could be known for its unique contribution to postwar culture.' The city council welcomed the debate but said history must sit alongside 'planning a prosperous future'.

Kevin McCloud, presenter of Channel Four's *Grand Designs*, said, 'Plymouth will be all the poorer if these buildings are not conserved for future generations'.

However, one city resident described the buildings as 'grey, bland concrete'.

Wet Weather

A mixed blessing: Plymouth has a temperate oceanic climate which is generally wetter and milder than the rest of England.

The Plympton Pong

The 'Plympton Pong' was the result of a breakdown in equipment at a Plympton sewage works in 2004, which led to a build-up of sludge. The resulting smell caused a pongy nuisance for local residents and is still remembered today.

Sir John Hawkins

England's first slave trader, John Hawkins made a good profit buying and capturing negro slaves in West Africa and trading them for gold and other valuables with the Spanish settlers across the Atlantic.

Views from Yesteryear

G.6181   THE SUN LOUNGE, PLYMOUTH.

GATEWAY ENTRANCE TO HOE, PLYMOUTH.

Things to do in Plymouth

Checklist

Tour the city in an open-top bus ☐

Try a Cap'n Special (fish burger) at Cap'n Jaspers on the Barbican ☐

Sip Plymouth Gin in The Refectory, the unique cocktail lounge situated in the historic Blackfriars Distillery ☐

Take one of the boat trips from Coxside – how about Fish 'n' Trips? ☐

Browse the indoor market ☐

Visit the Drake Circus shopping centre ☐

Stroll along Plymouth Hoe and enjoy the vistas across Plymouth Sound ☐

Climb Smeaton's Tower ☐

Catch the Cremyll Ferry to Mount Edgcumbe Country Park ☐

Sample a tasty pasty at Ivor Dewdney ☐

Enjoy a performance at the Theatre Royal ☐

See the marine life at the National Marine Aquarium ☐

Have a meal at the seventeenth-century China House on the Barbican ☐

Take in the spectacular views of the city and Plymouth Sound from the Wheel of Plymouth ☐

Go ice-skating or take in a show at the Plymouth Pavilions ☐

Visit the Plym Valley Railway – a must for steam enthusiasts ☐

Picture Credits

Unless otherwise stated, pictures are either by the authors or not in need of a credit.

Page:

Inside cover. Smeaton's Tower on Plymouth Hoe. (www.istockphoto.com)

2. Welcome to Plymouth.

3. Plymouth Coat of Arms.

7. Plymouth Hoe.

9. Plymouth city arms.

11. Pin Lane, the Barbican.

11. Castle Dyke Lane.

11. The former Pennycomequick public house.

13. Aerial view across the city.

15. Sir Joshua Reynolds, the Plympton-born painter and first president of the Royal Academy of Art. (www.istockphoto.com)

17. Street sign near Plymouth Railway Station.

21. Sign at the Gin Distillery, Southside Street.

21. Commemorative plaque and tree in the grounds of the fifteenth-century Prysten House, commemorating the visit of the Plymouth Michigan delegation to Plymouth in July 1970.

23. The Stars and Stripes fly alongside the Union Jack on the Barbican during the America's Cup, September 2011. The National Aquarium is in the background.

24. Plymouth Pier, *c.*1910.

25. Devonport Prison on Central Park Avenue, which closed in 1877.

26 & 27. Iconic view of Plymouth seafront. (www.istockphoto.com)

29. Freshly caught fish on sale at the Market Plaice in Plymouth's Pannier Market.

29. Brittany Ferry arriving into Plymouth.

29. Tinside Lido, Plymouth Hoe.

31. Plymouth Pier, destroyed in the 1941 Blitz.

31. City Museum & Art Gallery.

31. A Plymouth tram, early 1900s.

33. Graduates having their 'Class of 2010' photograph taken after a ceremony. (Courtesy of Lloyd Russell, University of Plymouth)

33. Drake Circus shopping centre.

33. Plymouth Theatre Royal.

33. The Minerva Inn pub sign on Looe Street.

Printed in Great Britain
by Amazon

78692451R00078